# Brew U2

## by Justine Shearstone

### Brewing Stronger Ideas in U

*Brew* **U2**

*Brew* **U2** by Justine Joy Shearstone

Books may be purchased in quantity by contacting ShearstoneMedia@hotmail.com.

Published by: Shearstone Media
Cover Design: Melissa Hudson/Shearstone Media

ISBN 978-0-692-4448-32

First Edition, 2015

Printed in the United States of America

www.justineshearstone.com

*Brew* **U₂**

*For my Father, Norm Herl, who taught me that strength, determination, love, and Heavenly guidance are the keys to **BREW**ing a rich and abundant life.*

*Brew* **U₂**

# Table of *Contents*

# Brew U2

# *Brew* U₂

# Brew U2

# *Brew* **U2**

## Who Inspires Your Do?

"What made you decide to write this book?"
"Why now?"
"How did you come up with this?"
"How did you go about publishing it?"

These are just some of the many questions that were posed to me after I wrote the first "Brew U." While they are all excellent questions, they also insinuate that someone or something drove me to do it. And yes, that is true. There are many factors that determined why I wrote the book, when I wrote it, and how I went about doing it. But I think the most important factor of them all is WHO inspired me to do it: my mother and my husband.

I did not think that I could write a book. I thought you had to have some special skill or technical ability. While I wrote for a living, I did not write books. I wrote articles. Scripts. Not books. Plus, I didn't have the time (or so I thought). But with my husband's constant encouragement and the passing of my mother, something finally clicked. It was no longer time to contemplate, it was time to do. It felt right to write. And to write right now.

This has me **BREW**ing about goals, dreams, and aspirations. Who or what has inspired *U* to go and do?

## Lucky Charms

It's St. Patrick's Day. Much of the office is decked out in green and making evening plans to celebrate, although I believe some of them will be starting a bit earlier than they plan.

The topic then turned to the luck of the Irish and good luck charms. I started to **BREW** as one woman showed me a bracelet that she has worn non-stop for the past two years. It is lined with three white beads and a simple charm hanging from it. She began wearing it the moment her mother was diagnosed with a health condition. Just recently, her mother received a wonderful report about her health and my co-worker now credits this bracelet as a good luck charm.

My husband told me today that I was his good luck charm. A very, very sweet gesture.

I, on the other hand, don't really rely on anything for luck. But I do rely on God for help with unanswered prayers, even answered prayers, guidance, healing, and providing for good times, too! I suppose that makes Him my lucky charm.

It's amazing what or whom we turn to for solace or for a spark in our daily lives. Do *U* have a good luck charm? What is it about that charm that is so important?

# *Brew* **U₂**

## Consistent Cravings

As I write this, my hometown Cleveland Browns are in first place in their division in the National Football League (a huge feat since they have not been in this type of situation in nearly 20 years).

Always known to be the losers of the division, their newfound momentum along with the city's excitement has been heart-warming for me, especially since I am no longer living in Ohio.

Cleveland has been craving this after years of turmoil, indecision, and lackluster play. What is the secret to their most recent success? I believe it is consistency. As a team, they have been consistent in their play. Consistent in their beliefs in each other. Consistent in their determination. The management team appears to be consistent.

Their consistency got me ***BREW***ing. Stay consistent and the course you are on is bound to change. Trying to lose weight? Stay consistent in your lifestyle choices. Looking to change jobs? Stay consistent in your action plans. Want to strengthen or mend a relationship? Stay consistent in your endeavor.

I crave consistency. For me, it's a peace of mind sort of thing. Do *U* crave consistency? Is there something in your life that needs to be more consistent? What can *U* do to satisfy that craving?

# *Brew* **U₂**

U + New

Today, I am embarking on a new life path. It is my last day at my Maine employer and I will soon be leaving the Pine Tree State and heading back to the Sunshine State to return to my career in broadcast media.

As I depart from what will soon be my "old" employer, I began to ***BREW*** over the "new" skills that will propel me both professionally and personally. These skills include:

• A new view on what it means to be kind to others. The mission of this Maine employer was to help those with intellectual and mental disabilities live and work in their communities. The kindness that I witnessed between the people we support and those that support them was immense.

• A new view on living simply. Some of the people who work and rely on this agency live simple lives and I have discovered that having much is all in your perception.

• A new view on embracing life. Be present always. Laugh. Love. Appreciate. Enjoy the little things.

I will bring these new views to my familiar surroundings in Florida. How do *U* approach new beginnings? With fear and anxiety or do *U* embrace the challenge?

# *Brew* **U2**

## No ExcUses

"Social media ate my homework." Or perhaps it should read, "Social media deleted my homework." You read that right. Forget "the dog ate my homework" excuses, we are clearly in a different time.

I recently read an article that highlighted just how much time people devote to social media and how everyday life events are becoming extinct due to society's newfound love of digital living.

Soon after reading that article, I began to **BREW** and started noticing just how much people are buried in their phones. I witnessed teens at a coffee shop who were working on a project together. It sounded as though this project's deadline was fast approaching. Every once in a while, one would look at their phone and would share a post that someone elsewhere had put online; completely distracting everyone from their real life obligations.

It's not just the young people. I have witnessed grown adults letting things fall by the wayside but they are certain to keep their digital connections intact. Missed deadlines? Projects only half done? Laundry or simple chores not completed? Yup – but social media accounts were tended to with urgency.

I despise the excuse, "I forgot" or "I ran out of time" when I can see that these same people are clearly remembering and finding the time to live digitally; disregarding their real life. I do find myself getting buried in my phone from time to time, but I am finding ways to set boundaries and acknowledge the real life before me.

Notice that the letter "*U*" is in the word excuse. It's not the technology's fault, it's how we use it.  You can't blame social media for deleting your real life. It's how you approach digital living.

No more exc*U*ses. What exc*U*ses do *U* despise? Or what exc*U*ses are *U* making?

*Brew* **U2**

## Treasure Chest

I am currently in the hunt for a cool keepsake box. One that can store all of the memories from my wedding. I kept one of everything from that day to put in this box: the coasters we gave the guests as gifts, the pom-poms that went with the centerpieces, my garter belt, the signs and love mementos from the tables, as well as the small charms, cards, and other sweet sentiments that Graham and I were given as gifts.

When I was a little girl, my mom had this pink box where she kept many memories of my childhood: report cards, finger prints, baby items and other treasured memories. As I *BREW*ed over this, I discovered where I get the whole keepsake box idea from.

We all have material things that we treasure. But more importantly, I will treasure these childhood and wedding memories in my heart: literally in my chest. It's the true treasure chest.

What material things do *U* treasure? And what non-material things do *U* treasure?

# *Brew* **U₂**

## Comm-U-nication

Do you find yourself communicating more or less these days?

I ask, only because I read a study that found that out of everything taught, parents want their children to learn how to communicate the most. I found this fascinating and not so surprising since we now live in a digital age – which is advancing by leaps and bounds, whether we want it to or not.

This got me ***BREW***ing. What does the word communicate mean nowadays? If you are sending a text or message via the social media route, is that still considered "communicating"? Or is communication face to face? Does the lack of human interaction mean that we are not communicating as much? Or are we communicating now more than ever because digital means are faster and in some cases, safer? As long as *U* are involved, does it matter either way?

While the definition may be changing, I still consider face-to-face communication the most important of all. I suppose it's because I value the emotion, the eye contact, and the voice inflection when it comes to in-person communication.

What does comm-*U*-nication mean to *U*?

# *Brew* **U2**

Are U Money Hungry?

"You can't expect money if you don't respect money."

When I heard that, you would have thought a brick landed right on top of my head! I was dumbfounded! That simple sentence has really changed the way I approach finances. And I am still trying to wrap my head around it, honestly.

This quote came from Joyce Meyer, a well-known television evangelist. During this particular segment, she was discussing money, debt, and finding new ways to think about money: not as a burden, but as a blessing.

Throughout life, we are always trying to get ahead. Make more money. Buy nice things. While some people go into debt to have nice things (me included!); others have been given the patience of waiting.

Often times, the people who wait, as well as those who give, are the ones who respect money the most. She also spoke of how waiting and honoring God's timing when it comes to a financial decision can often times lead to an even greater reward.

It got me ***BREW***ing as to how money hungry I am. Do I allow my thoughts and feelings to be too consumed by money? What kind of relationship do *U* have with money?

# *Brew* **U₂**

Regret, Repair, Repeat

Regret. It's a word that my husband and I agree to disagree about.

It all started when I asked him if he thought regret was a normal part of life. He said yes. I question that theory. And thus, our debate began. We went back and forth over whether or not regret was just a feeling, if every single living being actually has a regret, when a regret is really a regret and not just a bad decision, and the whole idea of free will and how it plays into regrets. I could go on and on, but I will spare you.

As I **BREW**ed about this entire topic, I looked up the word regret in several dictionaries. It was described as a feeling of sadness, repentance, or disappointment over something that has happened or been done. I personally am still trying to come to terms with when a regret is truly a regret and not just a bad decision, but that's for me to figure out.

Perhaps our debate should not have been about the word regret itself, but rather how we handle the aftermath of a bad decision, a disappointment, or a regret. What is learned from it; how do we repair our regrets? How do we keep them from repeating? And most of all, what do we get from experiencing it?

Do *U* think regret is a normal part of life? How do *U* handle feelings of regret?

# *Brew* **U₂**

## Light Bright

I might be aging myself; but do you remember Lite Brite?

Originated in 1967, it was a light box with small colored plastic pegs that you would fit into a panel. Based on the template you used, the pegs would be constructed in a way that would illuminate to create a lit picture. I remember as a kid how excited I would be when I would turn it on and see the picture I created.

There are people in my life that also have that same effect. While some have been known to bright up my day with a word, gesture, or gift; there are some people whose very presence makes me smile. Heck, even when I think about certain people, my mood instantly changes to the good.

I ***BREW*** about this is as I think of those who put smiles on my face and don't even know it. What have *U* done lately to brighten someone's day?

*Brew* **U2**

Home Sweet Home(s)

The time had come: it was time to move back to Florida after spending a few years in Maine.

I never thought I would move back to Fort Myers again after I left the first time, but I welcome the opportunity to return. It was a nice area. I met a lot of nice people and it's a great place to experience new opportunities and new life experiences. The background and the weather aren't too shabby either.

When I informed some of my friends of my return, the most popular response I received was "Welcome home." Having moved to Fort Myers fresh out of college and having lived there for 15 years before moving to Maine, I never really thought of Fort Myers as "home." Sure, my parent's place in Ohio was considered "home," and that was by default since that was where I was born and raised. Plus, it was a place where I was loved, nurtured and grew from a baby to a young adult.

Once I settled into Fort Myers out of college, I admit I never thought of Fort Myers as "home". It was always just a stopping point on the way to wherever I was going.

As I **BREW** about this, I am welcoming the idea of calling Fort Myers "home".

Just like my parent's house, it was here that I received love, nurturing, and a chance to grow and expand as I experience my adult years.

# *Brew* **U₂**

And it's a place where I still continue to grow. Other than your house, where do *U* call home?

# *Brew* **U2**

## Foolproof

My husband loves the word "foolish." He says it all the time. "Well, that's just foolish," he will exclaim.

We see foolish behavior all the time. There's the one I call "Foolish Focused:" he's that guy on the sports field that is flamboyant, the one that wants to be noticed.

Then there's the "Foolish Thinking": those are the people that you watch and you wonder why they do what they do. They seem to lack any sort of forethought. Why do they say what they say? Do they realize or even know what they sound like or appear like?

As I *BREW* about this, I find that lack of forethought is one of my biggest pet peeves. Sure, there are things in life that we are not aware of. Yes, there are certain mistakes we have to make in order to learn something so we don't make a foolish mistake. However, those who know they need to do or say something and don't – well, that's just plan foolishness.

What things do *U* find foolish?

# *Brew* **U₂**

## Musical Smells

I don't know about you but I love music.

I find that during certain times in my life, I tend to gravitate toward one style of music. As my circumstances change, or events change, I start listening to something completely different. But what's really strange, is that my nose knows, too. And this has me ***BREW***ing.

It's amazing how certain songs leave an imprint in our lives. I often associate certain 70's music with my mother. Not because she liked 70's music but because that is what would be playing as background music when she and I would spring clean the house. As a result, when I hear the 70's music, I can smell the window cleaner and the disinfectants.

Whenever I hear Elvis, I think of my father. As a little girl, I remember sitting in the passenger seat of his truck. For some reason, I always smell wood burning – probably because we cutting wood during the fall season.

When I hear smooth jazz, I think of Florida and instantly smell salt and ocean air. I remember fondly having dinner at a friend's house when I was first turned on to smooth jazz; they had the most beautiful house in a wonderful tropical surrounding.

Is there a musical style that *U* associate with? Or which songs best describe *U*?

# *Brew* **U2**

Who are U, really?

Who are *U*? Go ahead, think about it for a second.

OK. Now, who are *U*, really?

We did this exercise at work. We were asked to jot down who we thought we were individually. The leader read our answers randomly and anonymously. Some of the most popular answers: a good friend, honest, dependable, loving, etc.

Then the leader asked, "Who are you, really?" This time, we were given a longer time to jot down our answers. After several minutes, the responses were read randomly and anonymously again. This time, the answers were extremely different, almost negative: judgmental, self-absorbed, unhappy, uncertain, and insecure.

We talked about this briefly and why our answers changed to the negative when given more time for self-reflection. How much of it was the truth? How much of it was just our minds playing tricks on us? We began to *BREW*. The leader of the group then challenged us to tackle those negative feelings and the best ways to remedy them for the positive.

So, I ask U again, "Who are *U*, really?"

# *Brew* **U₂**

## Actions Scream Louder Than Words

I got to **BREW**ing about the phrase "Actions speak louder than words" after I witnessed a co-worker and her actions in the workplace.

She truly is one of the nicest people I have ever met in my entire life. Not only is she kind to everyone she comes in contact with (even those who aren't so nice to her), but her actions back up her intentions, even more so than her words.

Every day, she walks in with a smile and a warm greeting. But along with that friendly gesture, I notice how she handles her work tasks. Every single day she works hard. She is thorough. She follows through with tasks and with people as she promises. She goes above and beyond what she is supposed to do in a given day, while treating people with respect and kindness in the process.

She and I got to talking one day and I told her how much I admired her personality, her work ethic, and her integrity. I ended the conversation with, "Not only do you do what you say, but you say what you do." I am striving to role model her ways and do the same.

Her actions clearly scream louder than words. Do *U* know someone who does what they say? And also says what they do? Can *U* say the same about yourself?

# Brew U2

Lately, I have been drawn to programs that highlight people's success stories. Not only do I like to hear how they climbed the ladder of their own particular success, but who or what helped them to succeed.

Many of the ones I have heard or read credit their parents in one way or another. Most often, the parent is backing them, supporting their initiatives. However, there have been a few who have admitted that they went against the grain and pursued things their parents did not exactly agree with or their parents did not think it would be a good move for them.  In other instances a health concern, a moment in poverty, a proactive school teacher, or a life changing event propelled people to reach for their dreams.

No matter what the story or who helped to contribute to the achievements, most of the successful people attributed their goals to someone or some life event. I began to ***BREW*** over my paths to success.  My parents were prominent in establishing my work ethic. My mother's death and my husband's prompting helped me to write and publish a book.  There are countless of other people and situations I can credit for other successes in my life.

Who or what do *U* attribute to your successes in life?

# Brew U2

## Your Journey Begins

I had a lot of time to **BREW** during a drive from Maine to Florida. In fact, around 24 hours of deep thoughts and strange ramblings could be found churning in my head during that trip.

I looked around at the cars all headed the same direction as I was. Each vehicle going somewhere different, yet we were all sharing the same path to wherever our destination is. I began to look at the license plates to try and determine if they were local, long distance travelers like myself, and just what their travel plans would entail.

Then, a song by the rock group Journey came on the radio. As I listened, I began to actually focus on the word journey. Each person was on their own journey. Not just on the highway but also in life. You. Me. We are all on our own journeys. Our life journeys belong to us, each uniquely our own. In fact, the letter "*U*" is smack dab in the middle of the word journey! What a great way to remember to stay true to the journey and the life you want to lead.

What journeys do *U* have left to travel?

# *Brew* **U₂**

Raging Billboards

Another thing I ***BREW***ed about during a drive from Maine to Florida was the evolution of the billboard.

My, how they have changed. From standalone messages to rotating digital phenomenon, the push to get the message to you is clearly a massive feat. Interestingly, I didn't see any billboards until after I left Maine, since Maine doesn't promote the use of billboards.

But once I hit the border, BAM! There they were. All kinds of businesses promoting all kinds of products. Some businesses took on the task of sending you a different message every few miles along your journey, all in an effort to make sure you, the traveler, made that stop to indulge in their services.

Once I hit a stretch of roadway in North Carolina, it started getting ridiculous. At one point, I counted at least 10 billboards in one specific area, they were almost stacked on top of each other. I wonder if that really was the best use of money. It was almost as if they were yelling over each other with their large fonts and their flashy appearances.

Either way they wanted to get their message across and that got me ***BREW***ing. If you were a billboard, what would *U* look like? What would your message be?

# *Brew* **U2**

## Comfort Food Chains

Comfort food. What is the first thing you think of? Mashed potatoes? Pasta? Creamy, rich dishes? Perhaps it's a certain dessert? Whatever it is, everyone has their own version of comfort food.

I do, too. But lately, I've gone beyond "Mom's" comfort foods and have found myself gravitating toward certain foods from certain restaurants or shops.

While living in Maine, I found myself craving certain food chains that you could only find in the south. While living in Florida, I found myself wanting foods from certain restaurants in the northeast. It's a never ending cycle.

I began to **BREW** as to why I would crave these certain foods at certain times. Am I craving the company and the atmosphere of these places? Is there some other reason? I can't think of any – perhaps I really just like the food and there is no ulterior motive whatsoever.

Do *U* crave certain comfort food chains? And do *U* know why?

# *Brew* **U₂**

## Human Glass

I watched as the sun shined through paving a long trail of bright hues. The teal twinkling in the light as if it were winking at me. I was mesmerized at the light that shown through this unique piece of sea glass that was gifted to me.

You could not escape the bright, friendly resonance that was shining through this small, precious trinket. It was a tiny gift but it took over the whole room.

As I sat and observed this, I began to **BREW** about my own appearance. Do I shine brightly to others like this simple piece of sea glass? Can you see the light of God resonate through me?

How do *U* let your light shine through every day? Do *U* know someone who lights up a room?

# *Brew* **U₂**

## Guilty as Charged

Full disclosure: I understand how money works. While I did not pursue a financially-based career, I know what I need to know to get by, and what I don't know, I have good friends and business acquaintances that can address any question I have. However, I am having a hard time practicing what they preach, or following my own roadmap. I am still trying to figure out why. I know what I need to do. I just don't do it. And my financial life suffers.

I should also add: I don't have any trouble helping other people with money or handling their money if need be. Just my own.

I always have good intentions, though. I will set a goal, follow a plan then get going. I will go for a while and then I fall off the wagon. Go. Fall. Go. Fall. Then the guilt creeps in.  Then it turns into a vicious cycle: Go. Fall. Guilt. Go. Fall. Guilt. And with each rotation, the guilt gets larger and larger.

Most recently, I have begun to **BREW** about this and am asking for guidance from above to help me conquer this issue. As they say, knowing your problem is the first step toward a solution.

How do *U* handle guilt?

# *Brew* **U2**

## "Compete" Chaos

Competition: it's a part of almost every industry.

And it's everywhere. On TV. In papers and magazines. Online.

Businesses are doing all they can to win your business, and most of all defeat their competition.

I work in an industry that does that same. They go to intense lengths to make sure they are up on the competition. There are endless strategy meetings. Nonstop changes on the best ways to win. Who can deliver? Who can't? Do we need to bring in more people? How do we look? How do we sound? What is our message? Competing is first and foremost: it's "compete" chaos.

I heard one time that we are the CEO of our lives. I began to **BREW** about competition and got to thinking about how I use competition in my own life. I don't find myself competing with others as much as I do competing with myself! I am always trying better myself: do the right thing, lead the right lifestyle, be kind to others, but most of all, be kind to myself.

Who do *U* find yourself competing with? How do *U* deal with competition?

# *Brew* **U₂**

## The Difficult People

Are there people in your life that you consider to be difficult?

Some people have more than others, but I do believe that everyone has that one person that they simply have a hard time getting along with.

I have one in my life and admittedly, I sometimes cringe at the thought or mention of this person. With some unexpected changes in my life, I will be now be in contact with this person more than ever before. So, I have been **BREW**ing about this and am trying to deal with this inner irking in a more loving, positive, and constructive kind of way.

I am also trying to think about the people that I have good relationships with. Why do they work? How can I apply the characteristics of these relationships to the more difficult ones.

Who do *U* deal with the difficult people in your life? Is there something *U* can do to change that relationship?

# *Brew* **U₂**

## Val-U Meals

"Do you want to turn this into value meal?" was the question I was asked during a quick stop into a fast food restaurant.

I got to **BREW**ing about that question as I sat and ate the food I ordered. (I did not get the value meal.) The value meal is considered the "best deal" for your money. The intention is to make your dining experience even better because you are getting a combination of food at LESS cost. A BETTER experience. A VALUABLE one. I then noticed that the letter "U" is in value!

How do I val-U myself? Am I giving the best me to others? How am I making someone's experience better? How am I making my own life experiences val-U-able?

How do *U* value *U*?

# *Brew* **U2**

## Happy Places Means Happy Faces

What makes you happy?

For me, it's many things:
1) Drinking wine by a pool
2) Dinner at a waterfront restaurant
3) A Def Leppard concert
4) Key Lime Pie
5) Getting together with a good friend

These are just a few of what I call my happy places. Places, people, or moments that make me satisfied with life. They get me **BREW**ing. They get me motivated. Energized. But most of all, these happy places make me thankful. Thankful for the people in my life. Thankful for what I have been blessed with. Thankful for the simple moments.

Do *U* have a happy place? What makes *U* happy?

# *Brew* **U₂**

## "To Do U" List

I am the master of lists. I have to-do lists. I have backup to-do lists. I even have lists of lists!

It's getting rather ridiculous, but I am finding that without these lists, I would probably end up like a hamster in a wheel without accomplishing a single thing.

I read in a book that we shouldn't push ourselves to tackle everything on our to-do list. I began to ***BREW***. I agree with that – to a point. I think it's constructive to do at least something on your to-do list. I try to at least seek out to do something, if I know I am not going to get all of it done. And if I don't finish that one thing, then that's okay, at least I made some sort of headway.

But there is one thing on my to-do list that I accomplish each day – time for myself. Whether it's 5 minutes, an hour, or even a few. I need to do "me". Without putting me on the list, I am no good to anyone else, or myself really.

Are *U* part of your to-do list?

# *Brew* **U₂**

## Do U Hear What I Hear?

There's a radio station that I listen to often in Florida. Still do.

When I lived in Florida for the first time in my life, I met a man who was a DJ for that radio station. We became friends and still are to this day. Knowing the man behind the voice made listening to the station that much better.

While relocating back to Florida for the second time, I immediately turned on the radio station when I returned. It was strange. The same jingles. The same concept, but he was no longer a DJ there. It was like a piece of the puzzle was missing.

I began to **BREW** about the sounds we often hear that we don't even notice until they are gone. When I moved away from Florida and to Maine, I noticed the lack of birds in the cold Maine winters. I also noticed that sounds of the breezes in the trees had a different sound to them in the Maine summers as opposed to the rustling sounds that the palm trees make in Florida.

What sounds do *U* hear that bring joy to your life?

# Brew U2

## StUbborn

I am definitely a type-a personality.

Once I get an idea, thought, or strategy in my head, I spring into action. If I can't act yet, then I will think about it and think about it and think about it some more until I can actually take action. I suppose I fool myself into thinking that the act of thinking IS action.

This can be a blessing and a curse. On one hand, I can spring into action, get the ball rolling, and things are going smoothly and without delay. But, sometimes I tend to move too quickly without maybe going over all of the facts and figures. Or, in some instances, I get too focused on that one thing and dismiss any other possible ideas of approaching the issue.

I began **BREW**ing about this when I was faced with what I thought was a great decision yet it wasn't coming to fruition. After much agony, I have now learned that there was a better alternative had I not been so stubborn. I got in the way of my own stubbornness. Notice the letter "U" in the word stubborn?

Do *U* get ever get in your own way?

# *Brew* U2

## Growing Gains

As I write this, I am currently struggling with a huge challenge in my career.

I am **BREW**ing about this because the new job that I am at is requiring a complete change of mind and focus on my part. Things that I once knew in this arena have expanded by leaps and bounds. What used to be fun has now become a bit hectic due to these massive changes.

As I grow accustomed to these new challenges, I find myself doubting myself. Can I do this? Am I failing? Are my mental concerns over these challenges actually hindering me from keeping an open mind? And with these questions comes frustration, anxiety, fear, a severe sense of disappointment and lack of confidence on my part.

My husband has continued to reassure me that in time I will get it. And once I get it, I will excel. I just need to relax. Take it easy. Communicate with God, follow His word and encouragement and in due time, the lightbulb will click and I will be completely at ease. So, I am taking his advice.

And while it's tough, every time I get worked up, I try and focus my mind upward instead of inward. I guess I am going through what I will affectionately call, "Growing Gains".

In what area of your life are *U* experiencing "Growing Gains"?

# *Brew* **U₂**

Business Practices

While having lunch with a friend, the name of a co-worker came up. He said, "If you want to know anything about anyone, you go to her." We both laughed. It was completely accurate.

After that lunch, I began ***BREW***ing about all of the "busy bodies" we know in our lives. As I was sorting through all of the different people I knew, I realized that there were two kinds in my life:

1) Those who know all because they seek it out or engage in active knowledge and gossip sharing with others

2) Those who know a lot about people because they confide in them. These people don't share the information that is given, they just know because they are trusted with it.

The former are those that could start their own business about knowing everyone's business! The latter are those that I suspect would never want to have that sort of business.

I fall into both categories at times. Normally the information I share is more of the goofy type, which I am trying not to share altogether. However, if something deeply personal and important is shared, I do tend to keep it locked away.

# *Brew* **U2**

Which business practice do **U** fall into? Do **U** keep other people's information to yourself? Or do **U** tend to share too freely with others?

# *Brew* **U₂**

A Picture Worth a Thousand Thoughts

It was April 10th. It was National Siblings Day.

I scrolled as friends and colleagues posted childhood (and some adult) pictures of themselves with their siblings. It was fun to see how they looked when they were younger compared to how they look now. Some looked exactly the same! Others not so much. It was also neat to see the backgrounds and their surroundings at the time the picture was taken.

As I stared at these pictures, I started to **BREW** over the people's faces. I thought about what they looked like then and what their goals and aspirations may have been at that time. Then, I fast forwarded to now, what they are doing, where they are living, and most of all how their lives have unfolded.

I thought about a few of my own pictures as a kid. My hopes, dreams, thoughts, and "what I would grow up to be" then and how it has turned out now. What if everything I wanted came true? Would I be happy? Would I be miserable? No matter what did or didn't happen, I am happy with what I have, what I have experienced and who is in this life that I currently lead.

How do *U* view your childhood pictures now that *U* are grown up?

# *Brew* **U₂**

Nothing More than Feelings

I am battling with myself today.

The problem: what I am feeling is not what is being perceived. Let me explain. I am currently struggling to achieve something at work that I believe is extremely important. But this process is going slower than I think it should. Those around me think otherwise. They say I am going at the right pace and that I am not going to get it all at once. It takes time.

What has me **BREW**ing is that I used to be able to do what it is that I am trying to achieve. The whole "it's like riding a bike" theory is not quite what it is in this situation. Yes, OK, others around me say I need time. Internally, I am going crazy because I know I can do this and that time shouldn't be a factor. It should be innate. It should be natural. And currently, it's not.

A friend told me to stop letting my feelings get in the way of my progress. Instead, pray and be faithful. I am trying to do that. But every once in a while, I find my feelings trying to get in the way of my faith and have to try and erase them.

Do *U* let feelings get in the way of faith?

# *Brew* **U₂**

## Royalty Loyalty

I am very fortunate to have many friends that I can also call loyal friends.

I am a very loyal person as well, so I treasure those people that are loyal in return. Those that carry the "loyal" title are those that I hold very dear and also very high on my list. I admire them.

I am **BREW**ing about this after watching a show about the British Royals. While they command attention around the world and they have a huge fan base, I find that I look up to my loyal friends as if they are royalty in their own right.

These "royals" are fair. Just. They look out for my best interest. They are not afraid to tell me the truth. Similar to those who are considered traditional royalty, I hold them in very high esteem. I listen to them with intention. I know they have my best interests at heart. They are rare in this day and age. Which is probably why I hold them so close to my heart.

Do *U* have a royal loyal or two in your life?

# *Brew* **U2**

Influences for Every Occasion

Who are your influences when making decisions?

I am **BREW**ing about this as I was faced with a major decision in April 2015. I found myself in a situation that I have never been in before and this decision was going to affect the rest of my entire life, and my finances as well. I wanted to make the most informed and educated decision.

I sought out advice from everyone I could think of. My father. A few friends. People who are currently in the situation in that I am having to make a decision about and a host of other people whose advice would qualify.

I also have been actively seeking information and guidance from God. I know He will have my best interest at heart. But as far as earthly beings, I am fortunate to have smart family members and friends.

As it is with everyone, I rely on certain influences depending on the decision I have to make. With major financial decisions, I tend to consult my husband, father, and other financial savvy friends. As for other less important decisions, I have an influence for each topic.

Do *U* have an influence for every occasion? Who influences *U*?

# *Brew* **U2**

## Support System

I have a great husband.

I am **BREW**ing about this because he always has my back. He's an encourager. He listens (or acts like he does). He's fair. He's honest. Trustworthy. Loving. He's my best friend. He's the ultimate support system.

Before we were married, I was always considered the independent one. He says that is one of the things that attracted me to him. Sure, I would call on my parents for advice here and there, but after we got married that all changed. Now, as I grow older, I find myself relying on my husband now and sometimes more than myself. (I hope this doesn't mean he will like me less!)

I gravitate to him now when faced with a decision, issue, thought or concern. He does the same for me. I love that I can have a support system that I can call on in a pinch; that will not judge, criticize, or belittle me in any way.

Who do *U* consider to be part of your support system?

# *Brew* **U₂**

## Attention Getters

How many apps do you have on your smartphone? How many new apps have you downloaded since receiving that phone?

As the saying goes, there truly is an app for that! There's an app for finding the best gas prices. Restaurants have apps. Stores have apps. Everything that you can possibly think of has an app. There's even an app you can download for amusing reading while using the restroom!

This app thing got me to ***BREW***ing. People love apps so why aren't humans like apps? Let me explain:

Apps are designed to be ready when you are. You touch. It performs. Are you ready at a moment's notice to help someone in need? They also are also designed to give us answers to prices, deals, services, etc. Are you giving your best when it comes to family, friends, work, and other ventures?

App creators put a lot of thought and time into making sure apps are pleasing to the eye and easy to navigate. Are you welcoming to people? Do *U* take the time to present yourself in the most admirable light? Do *U* take much thought in how you interact with others?

What if there was an app specifically designed about *U*? What would it look like? What service would *U* provide?

# *Brew* **U₂**

## Celebrate U

Sure, we celebrate birthdays, anniversaries, weddings, baby showers, bridal parties, but when was last time you celebrated U?

I don't mean a birthday. I mean a sincere thought provoking celebration recognizing your accomplishments, your hopes, your dreams, your over-comings, and most of all just being U.

I ***BREW*** about this because I find that I tend to focus on what is going wrong and not taking time to celebrate what is going right. Yes, I pray for favor. I pray for peace. I pray for guidance. I celebrate what God has done for me, but I think it's important to celebrate myself. What I have become. What I bring to my family, friendships, my community, and society as a whole.

I am now going to carve out time throughout the year to take on this idea of celebrating me. My celebration will include doing something I thoroughly enjoy, listing my gratitude's, recognizing my accomplishments, focusing on what I have done and how it will help me in the future. I will most likely top it all off with a piece of cake. Because cake to me is a celebration in itself!

How do *U* celebrate *U*?

# Brew U2

## Look Up

It was horrible pain. I woke up one morning and went to move my head to look up and the pain came shooting from my shoulders. I realized I had one of those nights where I slept wrong.

I am sure you have had those nights. You wake up and are miserable the rest of the day having to deal, and readjust to wherever your pain lies. It can be a nuisance. Frustrating. And it can affect your entire day.

In my instance, I spent much of the day with my head down. Barely looking straight ahead. It only lasted for about a day or two and I was fine. But during those rough 36 hours I was reading in a magazine about the power of looking up and how it can lift our spirits, reenergize us, and give us hope. I began to **BREW** about this. I wished I could look up, but I couldn't due to my physical pain, but what was even better was that I could look up mentally if I needed to. And that was really all that I needed. That certainly was no pain in the neck!

I began to think about the people in my life who don't believe in a high power or God or anything of faith. They have no desire to look up or don't know the power of looking up. How empty life may be because that promise of hope, peace, and excitement is not even an option to them.

How do *U* refocus when pains creep up in your life?

# *Brew* U2

## Double Vision

I had one of those moments that happens to all of us at one time or another. I was looking at a picture that I was very familiar with, when all of a sudden, I saw something in the picture I had never seen before. I had to do a double take.

After I let my new discovery settle in, all I could see was that new area of the picture I had never noticed before. Now when I look at it, I think, 'how did I miss that?' because it was an extremely valuable part of the picture.

My vision was renewed. I began to **BREW** about this and thought about all of the things in my life that I tend to miss in the details. If I have a bad day, I tend not to pay attention to all of the things that went right, only the wrong. Or if I am having one of those silly feeling-sorry-for-myself moments, I fail to think about all of the positives in my life.

I am blessed. I need to start doing double takes more often. Better yet, I need to have double vision. A way to see the positive picture through the heavy fog of negativity. Right myself when I feel myself headed in the wrong direction.

What do *U* do to combat negativity?

# *Brew* **U₂**

### Do Over

I have worked in the TV industry and it is a fascinating one.

There's a lot of thinking on your feet especially in news where things are happening so rapidly. News is arriving and you are competing against the clock to get it on the air in a timely manner that makes sense to the viewers.

Aside from the "live" element, there are also times when things are pre-taped. Those are the most luxurious moments. If you mess up, you just stop and re-record it. This can happen again and again depending on the day. Regardless, you can do it as perfectly as you want. Do-overs can happen whenever you want them to.

I started **BREW**ing about this during a recent taping session. I began thinking about times in my life where I wish I could have just said, "Stop! Let's do it over." Of course, this can't happen so I have to learn how to take my "live" moments the best I can, make the most of them, and find a new way of dealing with it if the situation arises again.

Are there times in life when *U* wish *U* could have a do-over?

# *Brew* **U₂**

## Space Invaders

What does your space say about *U*?

I was watching a talk show and they were trying to set up a single woman with a good guy. In a twist on the old dating game, they let the gal look into the guy's homes to see how they live. Based on what she saw and what her gut instinct said, she picked the guy that matched the particular home she liked best.

These homes were vastly different. One was very pristine, with lots of crystal, diamonds, and all of the things that many girls love. The second home had more of a rugged feel. There were work tools in the living room, sports related items in the bedroom and so on.

When asked, the girl picked the guy with the pristine home. So, they brought out the gentleman with the rugged home first so she could meet him before she met the "winner". The "loser" in this instance was a nice looking guy. You could tell she may have regretted her decision. Then they brought out the "winner". I think she was okay with her decision, but her reaction to the second guy was not as positive as the first.

 I began to **BREW** when I saw how each of the guys actually did match their spaces. The pristine guy was nicely dressed and appeared as though he liked the finer things in life. The blue collar guy seemed very down to earth and simple.

# *Brew* **U₂**

It's amazing how much we assume what people might be like based on the space they live in. Does your space match *U*?

# *Brew* **U₂**

## Past Lives

If I have learned anything in the past year, it is how to try and embrace patience.

I **BREW** about this because I find that I am impatient when it comes to things I have control of. Such as finding the right house to buy, saving for a big purchase, things like that. I find that my patience is limited. I want the people, events or calendar days to hurry. I am working on that.

However, when it comes to things I don't have control of, I have extreme patience. Delayed flight? No problem. Traffic jam? So what. Bad weather? Oh, well. While I may find these things a nuisance, I don't become impatient, I just go with the flow.

It doesn't seem to make sense to me. But it's what I have learned and now I just have to learn how to deal with it better.
What have *U* learned in the past year?

# *Brew* U₂

## Miracle Workers

Working in news, I am bombarded with stories every day. They could be uplifting, tragic, puzzling, disgusting, annoying, even frustrating.

But no matter the plethora of stories, there's always one where a miracle has occurred. I ***BREW*** about this because it amazes me every time. One I remember fondly is a motorcyclist who lost control of his ride, flipped over a bridge and landed on a parked SUV below.

In that SUV, was a mother and her son who had pulled into that parking space below to double check directions to the event they were headed to. They were unhurt, but of course, surprised.
Imagine: how many times have you pulled over for an instant? Probably many. Now what are the odds that a bike comes out of the sky and lands on your car? Probably not many. And that the fact that they weren't hurt, is indeed, a miracle.

Its stories like these that renew my faith in a world where it seems all faith is lost.

What miracles have *U* witnessed lately?

# *Brew* **U₂**

Balancing Act

Like you, I have seen and experienced bouts where I feel like I am working non-stop. Then there are other times where I feel like I am basking in relaxation (although those are very few and far between).

Mix in technology these days, and it makes it even harder to separate the two. I ***BREW*** about this as I set out on a task to look something up for work. I almost immediately get distracted in my search and start to wander to other things online that are not work-related.

 Before the days of instant tech gratification, I was able to separate work and pleasure with no problem. Now, I have to step up my disciplinary skills a notch and actually remove technology from the working equation whenever possible.

Unless it's absolutely necessary, I will avoid technology like the plague. I will intentionally force myself not to go online. Have errands to do around the house? Hit the gym? Run an errand? No scrolling online until it's finished. It's actually been great because it has helped me to be in the present much more. I look forward to work in order to earn the pleasure.

How do *U* balance work and pleasure?

# *Brew* **U2**

## The Daily U

I often hear parents bragging about their kids, their child's accomplishments and that's great. But some of the parents don't breathe a word about what is going on in their own lives.

I get it. Having kids takes up a lot of time. A lot of energy. And yes, to some parents, their kids are their lives. But before the kids came, that parent had a life. Why should that take a backseat just because there was a decision to bring another life into the world?

I ***BREW*** about this after seeing several posts like these on Facebook. I see a lot of: Junior did this. Junior did that. I think of the parent who posts those things and the sacrifices they've made so Junior can achieve these things. What have the parent's achieved in the process? Have they had any time for themselves? Are they just not the bragging kind or have they just put their life on hold?

I am not knocking parenting. I have never been one and I admire those who are. I just hope some parents make the time for themselves. It will only help Junior in the process and will model the importance of individuality.

Do *U* put *U* in your daily schedule?

*Brew* **U2**

### Great Expectations

My husband took me to Montreal for our first anniversary.
I loved it. He loved it. We had a great time.

I had traveled to France 15 years earlier, but having the
opportunity to re-connect with French-Canadians was a real
treat. I treasure the culture, their way of life, even the way
they eat, drink, and socialize.

I *BREW* as I think back on how happy I am to have
experienced this with my husband. Just simply
experiencing new things with him yet knowing that
familiarity was only a border away in the States. My
experience far surpassed my expectation.

Upon returning, I was ready to get back into the groove of
life. For me, experiencing new things adds depths to my
mundane life. It shakes up my focus. It is refreshing.
I know some people who get very uncomfortable when it
comes to change. They hate getting out of their own
rhythm. The more their life can stay the same, the more
they will stay sane.

Do *U* like to experience new things or do *U* like to stick
with the familiar?

# *Brew* **U₂**

## The 6 Letter Word: H-e-a-l-t-h

Mention the word "health" and what comes to mind? Neglect? Disgust? Enjoyment? Dread? Willingness to change? Happiness? Serenity?

I ***BREW*** about this as I think about the health of the people I know. It's no secret that our health can change in an instant: a tragic accident, a diagnosis, an unexpected event. Then there's the health that can change over time: weight loss, weight gain, aging, neglect.

As I get older, I treasure my health more and more in regards to what sort of control I have over it. I see how purposely unhealthy habits can affect people, including myself. I am not me when I am unhealthy, I am a different version of me one that I would rather not get to know anytime soon. So I try to stay in control of the things I can control.

What does the word health mean to *U*?

# *Brew* **U₂**

## Dress for Success

It has been said that you should dress for the job you want, not the job that you have.

There's some truth to that, but I think dressing for success is not just outward, but inward. There's the mental dressing as well.

No matter what I look like on the outside, my mental wardrobe matters. Without positivity, confidence, and stability, I might as well be naked. I can surely be a mess in a nice dress.

I **BREW** about this after hearing a friend comment on how excited she was to wear a dress. This dress didn't always fit her, she had to lose weight to fit into it. Not only was she dressed in her favorite dress, she was mentally dressed. And it showed.

Yes, her body may have looked great, but it was her mental attitude and positive outlook that really made the outfit. The clothes are just the accent piece.

How do *U* dress for success?

# *Brew* U2

## Rules of Ignorance

Some people I know find my frustration with technology annoying.

I **BREW** about this especially when I see people who live their lives looking down at their devices rather than looking forward at life.

I do use technology – a lot – but not as much as some people I know. I do look at Facebook. I scroll through Twitter. I browse the news headlines on my phone. I bank online. Yes, I even use apps. But I do break the rules when it comes to reliance on technology.

I understand that technology is a part of our daily lives. We use it for work and for other needs. But we don't need it for everything!

I will intentionally put my phone away (gasp!) to spend more time with my husband. I will turn off my phone when I watch a TV show or movie or play a game with the family. I don't let technology rule my life – and that is one rule I am happy to break! I rule over my technology use.

What rules do *U* ignore?

# Brew U2

## Poll-U-tion

Who or what are the pollutants in your life?

We all have people, places, or things that leave ugly residue in our lives. I **BREW** about this as I think back on one person in my life whose personality left such a bad taste in my mouth that whenever I think about that person, I shudder.

Whenever a situation comes up that reminds myself of this person, it's like a dark cloud lingers overhead. The air feels polluted. I do everything I can to try and clear the air. I turn to positive thinking. I am immediately grateful that I am not like this person. I focus on the good people and the good things around me.

I also notice how some people's pollutants tend to take over their atmosphere. And then there are others whose lives are better, clearer, because of the way they have cleared the air from the pollutants in their midst.

How do *U* clear the air of your pollutants?

# *Brew* **U₂**

Celebrities Among Us

Robert De Niro.

No, I don't know him but I know someone who looks just like him. They will remain nameless to protect the innocent (and maybe the offended).

After this look-a-like was pointed out to me, I did see similar behavioral traits as well. It really took all my energy to not laugh out loud every time I interacted with this particular person. I am not sure how this person would feel about these observations.

If I was told I looked like a celebrity, I am not sure what I would to. I may become too self-conscious but I suppose it all depends on the celebrity. If that particular celebrity was stuck up or snobbish, I certainly would not welcome the comparison. If they were known to be loving, giving, influentially positive, then I am all for it!

This has me *BREW*ing. Rather than being compared to a celebrity, how I can achieve star status in my own neighborhood through good deeds and civility?
I would much rather be remembered for those actions.

Do *U* know someone who looks or acts like a celebrity?

# Brew U2

Revise. Reinvent. Repeat.

It's a constant in my world.

As technology evolves, life lessons change, and demands increase, the only things that remains constant is the need to reinvent myself.

I've had to reinvent how I approach friendships. And I **BREW** over this since my recent job change called for some major reinvention. While it can be tough, I embrace the change and the chance to reinvent and evolve as much as possible.

The idea of learning about my strengths and weaknesses is a welcome challenge. It is difficult and freeing all at one time. Weeding away old ideas and thoughts in order to grow new roots can be invigorating. I won't say it is easy. But once you come to terms with the possibility of change, the change itself is not so bad.

So, how do I reinvent myself? With an open mind and triple amounts of prayer! Guidance, determination, soul-seeking and embracing what I do not know in order to learn are the best ways that I have learned so far to reinvent myself.

How do *U* reinvent yourself?

*Brew* **U₂**

## Dinner Plans

"Only hire people you want to have dinner with."
I read that in a magazine. This was the advice of a fashion designer who was discussing out to weed out underperformers in the workplace.

This had me ***BREW***ing. Would my current boss want to have dinner with me? If not, I am glad he didn't take on this designer's advice!

Then I began to ***BREW*** over people in my personal life. Especially those that I may allow to frustrate me. Why do I give them so much of my mental time and energy? I certainly don't want to have dinner with them so why are they taking up so much space? I need to just focus on the people that I want to have dinner with.

And what about those that you want to have dinner with but probably never will? Where do they fall?

Who do *U* tend to focus your time and energy on? Are they worth a place at your table at dinnertime? Do they fit the bill?

# *Brew* **U₂**

## Bad Break-Up

It is the break-up I never saw coming.

You would think that working on the overnight shift would involve tremendous amounts of coffee. But it didn't. The nature of my work involves little time to linger over cups of coffee. We barely have enough time to eat, so we just pick. Coffee unfortunately, doesn't take center stage.

It was somewhat of a sad realization. Especially since lingering over coffee is how these *Brew* **U** books came to be!

I began to ***BREW*** about my break-up with coffee. By the time I left work, hit the gym, did the errands, there simply wasn't time for my beloved java. We would have to reconnect on the weekends. And we do. I now linger over the coffee with my husband a little longer than usual; it's the time I look forward to after a hectic week.

Before this change in java schedule, I wondered if I was drinking too much coffee during the week. All it took was a small change to break-up a questionable habit and put it back into a more healthy perspective.

How do *U* break up with bad habits?

# *Brew* **U2**

## Mirror Image

When you look in the mirror, what do U see?

Old age? Youthfulness? Confidence? Worry? Exhaustion? Happiness? Sadness?

I began ***BREW***ing about this after I saw an ad in a magazine. It was promoting a new lipstick and the makers of it were touting that this new lip liner glides on so easily that you don't need a mirror to put it on.

Don't need a mirror? Could I survive without a mirror altogether? We rely on mirrors to make sure we are put together: does the hair looks good? Do our clothes match? Do we look presentable? But more and more, I see women looking at mirrors as a way of judging themselves.

At clothing stores, I hear women complain about their bodies in the dressing room. Rather than focusing on the dress just not being right, they blame their own bodies for not fitting into the dress! Their hips are too big for the dress. No, perhaps the dress just isn't the right cut for that particular body type.

I am trying to not fall into that trap. My quest is to use the mirror as a guide, not as a defining entity in my life. What do *U* see in the mirror?

# *Brew* **U₂**

Mission Possible: *U*

Businesses have mission statements. Why don't people?

While reading the mission statement at my own workplace, I began to **BREW** over my own personal mission statement. I am still trying to hash it out.

There's so much to consider: What IS my mission? How do I measure my mission and its success? What qualities do I need to sustain my mission?

Want to try and figure out yours?

Here's a roadmap of sorts that I found while doing some research online.

How do *U* want to be described?

What is your legacy?

What matters most?

What makes *U* feel happy and most fulfilled?

There *U* have it. Mission Possible: *U*.

*Brew* **U2**

## ABOUT THE AUTHOR

*Justine Shearstone is an Executive Producer, Writer, and Marketing Executive.*

*Helping people discover and achieve their true potential is her greatest passion.*

*Justine's deep-rooted conversations and experiences have led her to the beaches of Florida, the snowy mountains of Maine, and everywhere in between.*

*Justine is married to Graham and is the Stepmother of his two children, Ben and Alexis.*

*Brew* **U₂**

# Enjoy the Entire Series

# *Brew* **U**

 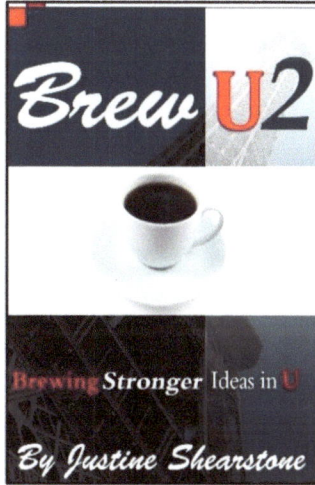

www.ingramcontent.com/pod-product-compliance
Lightning Source LLC
LaVergne TN
LVHW010027070426
835513LV00001B/4